I LOVE From DAUGHTERS OF FAITH

DEBBIE SALTER GOODWIN

Beacon Hill Press of Kansas City
Kansas City, Missouri

Copyright 1998
by Beacon Hill Press of Kansas City

ISBN 083-411-7282

Printed in the
United States of America

Cover Design: Mike Walsh

All Scripture quotations not otherwise designated are from the *Holy Bible, New International Version*® (NIV®). Copyright © 1973, 1978, 1984 by International Bible Society. Used by permission of Zondervan Publishing House. All rights reserved.

Permission to quote from the following copyrighted versions of the Bible is acknowledged with appreciation:

The *New King James Version* (NKJV). Copyright © 1979, 1980, 1982 Thomas Nelson, Inc. Used by permission.

The Living Bible (TLB), © 1971. Used by permission of Tyndale House Publishers, Inc., Wheaton, IL 60189. All rights reserved.

Library of Congress Cataloging-in-Publication Data
Goodwin, Debbie Salter
    Lessons of love from daughters of faith / by Debbie Salter Goodwin.
        p.   cm.
     ISBN 0-8341-1728-2 (pbk.)
     1. Women in the Bible. 2. Christian women—Religious life.
    I. Title
BS575.G68   1998
220.9′2′082—dc21

97-30451
CIP

10 9 8 7 6 5 4 3 2 1

*Dedicated to my mother,
Imogene Salter,
who mothered me with all her heart,
who took me to Jesus often,
who cried to God over my suffering,
who passed on to me the Word of life in such a way
as to create in me a love affair with God
that will not die.
I will always call you blessed.*

TABLE OF CONTENTS

The Mothers Who Brought Their
  Children to Jesus 7

The Daughter Who Answered
  Her Mother's Prayer..15

The Mothers Who Passed
  on the Good News 23

The Mother Whose Daughter Suffered 31

The Daughter Without a Mother..............................38

The Mother Who Learned to Laugh........................46

THE MOTHERS WHO BROUGHT THEIR CHILDREN TO JESUS

Some mothers were bringing their children to Jesus to bless them (Mark 10:13a, TLB).

Mothers are always taking their children somewhere. To school. To the doctor. To the store. To birthday parties. To church. Sometimes it's easy to think that a mother is little more than calendar keeper and chauffeur. Who knows what errands these Judean mothers had completed with babies on their hips and toddlers at their heels when they stopped to see Jesus. No doubt some of them were there on purpose. Perhaps others followed the crowd. Whatever brought them to this meeting with Jesus was not as important as what they did when they arrived.

THEY BROUGHT THEIR CHILDREN TO JESUS

They brought their children to Jesus. This was nothing new. Mothers were always bringing their children to the rabbis for a blessing. Rabbis blessed everything from new pots to pets. I'm sure most mothers made sure their children received every blessing possible. Blessed children were protected children. And a mother will do anything to protect her child.

When these women brought their children to Jesus, they didn't really understand what they were doing. He was a new teacher—perhaps He had a new blessing that their children had not received. They did not know they brought their babies to the very Son of God. That their children sat in the lap of the Creator.

THE DISCIPLES' INTERFERENCE

The disciples almost got in the way. Did they see all children as interruptions or just these children? Were they frustrated because their private conversation took second place to a lap full of children? Were they simply protecting Jesus' needs without sensitivity to the children's needs? Whatever their reason, they tried to keep the mothers and their children away from Jesus.

There will always be someone or something that can keep our children away from Jesus. But as mothers, our job is not to run interference. Our job is simply to take our children to Jesus. That's all these mothers did. Jesus did the rest. He took care of the disciples' misunderstanding by overriding their rebuke. Jesus will always be there to push back the people who would threaten to keep your children from Him. He makes it as easy as He can for anyone to get to Him. He will not, however, override your child's choice. That's why an early introduction to Jesus is so important. When a child grows up familiar with the lap of Jesus, he or she grows up knowing where true security is.

ACTING WITH THE DISCIPLES' IGNORANCE

It's one thing for others to keep our children from Jesus, but sometimes we act with the disciples' ignorance. While no God-fearing mother intends to keep her children away from Jesus, she can be a part of the separating distance. Busyness can reorder priorities and send mixed signals. Requiring transparent honesty from a child without modeling it confuses. The Bible pictures of self-control, forgiveness, and faith are difficult to transplant into a young life without a home picture to go with it. No parent will be perfect, but any parent growing in the fruit of the Spirit will be effective.

THE INVITATION OF JESUS

To settle the misunderstanding, Jesus tells the disciples to "Let the children come" (Mark 10:14,

TLB). That's all the invitation that these mothers and children needed. This was not the time when the mothers had to fight to get help for their children. Even the people who tried to keep them away did not stop His invitation. When the children were close enough to hear His invitation, it was easy for them to climb onto His lap.

Isn't that our responsibility as mothers—to take our children close enough to Jesus so they can hear His invitation? We need to be careful that our words don't get in the way. We need to learn how to take our fears to Jesus before we act out of fear and push children away. Remember, it was Jesus' rebuke and invitation that closed the gap. The mothers only brought their children to Jesus.

RELEASING OUR CHILDREN TO JESUS

There is only one thing to do with a child when you stand before Jesus. Release him or her into His arms. It's one thing to place a baby in the adoring arms of someone who inflates your pride over a newborn. It's quite another to practice the heart-wrenching releases between infancy and adulthood. While releasing our children to Jesus may be the most secure thing for them, it often attacks every fiber of a mother's desire to do all the protecting herself. We dare not render our children defenseless to live in the secular world, but we cannot throw them to a den of lions either. That's where every mother must understand there is only so much her hands and voice can do. That's when she learns to take her children to Jesus.

I have met mothers who were afraid of releasing their children to Jesus. Out of fear, they controlled, manipulated, and often isolated their children. Trying to meet every need of their children, they missed the one important one—the need to find security outside of a parent's hold. But when a mother isn't secure in the love of Jesus, she cannot pass on what she does not have. The mother who takes *herself* to Jesus knows firsthand the power of His blessing. She understands that her child's first line of defense is Jesus. No one advocates for your child more than He. No school counselor, no teacher, no doctor, no book author. And yet, too often, we reserve Jesus as the last resort instead of the first advocate. Whether the issue is toilet training or learning the alphabet, first date or marriage crisis, learning to take our children to Jesus first puts us in a better place to access other professional help.

WELCOMING CHILDREN

Children always change someone's agenda. They interrupt sleep, routines, conversations, and peace and quiet. Just as soon as we have adjusted to one stage of interruptions, another begins. Jesus did not see the children as an interruption. He saw them as the kingdom of God. He welcomed their innocence and trust and simple joy. He told His disciples to make time for the children.

We need to do the same. Making time and taking time are companion habits we need to practice. Making time involves specifically planning an activity or outing. Taking time means we lay aside another important activity to place a child's need before one of our own. Hyperactivity aside, the child who needs attention interrupts often. Frustrated by the many interruptions, we can miss the need. Learning to discern between the selfish interruption and the needy one requires a wisdom God knows how to give generously.

THE BLESSING

While the mothers brought their children to Jesus, it was Jesus who invited them into His lap. To receive the blessing, the children had to accept the invitation. Mark 10:16 describes the forceful way Jesus embraced these children: He "folded them in His arms."* This was no sweep of the hand or pat on the head. This was not a ritual blessing as the rabbis gave. When the children were close enough to touch, they were pulled even closer to His heart. Individually and with a fervent intention that caused all to pause, Jesus put His hand on them and blessed them.

There is always blessing in the touch of Jesus. As people came to know who Jesus was and what He could do, they were always pushing to get close enough to touch Him and receive His touch. These children knew nothing more than a friendly lap and a gentle hand. Yet they experienced the blessing of Jesus. He affirmed their worth. He honored their unique contribution. He made others take notice of their importance. He welcomed them.

In all the scheduling and chauffeuring and feeding and dressing we do for our children, do we see their importance as Jesus did? Are they an image of the kingdom of God to us? Do we welcome them as those valued by Jesus, even when they change our agenda? When we do, we share their blessing.

POLISHING OUR ROUGH EDGES

No crisis has challenged my Christian growth as much as motherhood. It exposes all my rough edges. Like rough, jagged rocks bouncing against each other to polish one another, children are gifts of God sent to polish their mothers. To resist is to keep the sharp points that can hurt myself and my child.

A MOTHER'S ONLY HOPE

Over and over, in the physical and emotional crises that punctuate childhood, mothers can take their children to Jesus. There are times when children will not get to Jesus unless mothers take them. And it is good to remember that children are never too old to be taken to Jesus. Whether they are 5 or 55, Jesus wants to bless their child-heart. What peace a mother has when she knows her child rests where the protection of Jesus knows no limit. Be assured that Jesus will always tell the children to "Come," and He will always rebuke anyone who would stand in their way. Be a mother who takes her children to Jesus.

---

*Ralph Earle, *The Gospel of Mark* (Grand Rapids: Zondervan, 1957), 125.

THE DAUGHTER WHO ANSWERED HER MOTHER'S PRAYER

[Miriam] stood at a distance to see what would happen to him (Exodus 2:4).

Stories abound about a mother's ingenuity to protect her children. A mother will fight wild animals, defy weapons, ignore personal pain, and exhibit unheard of energy to protect the child that has grown from her heart. That's why the story of Moses' mother, Jochebed, seems so contemporary. She, with the bravery of the Hebrew midwives, defied the execution decree and protected her son.

Can you imagine the fear that Jochebed's pregnancy brought? Hiding began early by trying to mask morning sickness and a growing bulge. Then she contended with muffling newborn cries and a restless infant. This went on for three months. When it became too dangerous to hide the baby at home, this resourceful mother came up with a plan. Perhaps the plan grew from her thoughts when she cradled her baby within her body. Perhaps she found out that a rocking baby was a quiet baby, and a quiet baby was a safe baby in Egypt. However the idea came, she prepared a waterproof basket to hold her newest treasure.

But how could she hide the basket, watch it daily, and still carry on responsibilities at home without inviting questions? A mother's need to be two places at once is not a new dilemma. And that's where Miriam comes in.

AN ANSWER TO PRAYER

Miriam was the answer to her mother's prayer. She is the first recorded baby-sitter. No baby-sitter ever had a more important job. She was not just to take care of her brother; she was on duty to save his life. It was natural for the older sister to be a little mother. After all, mothering a real live baby is more fun than rocking a rag doll. However, she did not understand that when she protected her brother, she protected the future of her family. Sometimes an answer to prayer reaches farther than first thought.

Being an answer to prayer is not easy. For Miriam, it meant more than listening for her brother's cry. She had to think quickly when Pharaoh's daughter threatened her brother's hiding place. She came up with a plan that answered a prayer her mother didn't even know to pray. Miriam restored her brother to her mother's arms, under the very nose of the pharaoh who had decreed his murder.

Miriam was the daughter who was willing to be there. She made sure the pitch held. She kept the basket from a reckless ride down the river. She found ways to stifle the cry of boredom and hunger. Miriam saved her brother's life and touched her mother's heart.

A MOTHER'S PRAYER

What prayers that mother must have prayed. Prayers for safety. Prayers for wisdom. Prayers for ingenuity. Prayers for hope in the face of overwhelming circumstances. Prayers that she, with all of her mothering, could not answer. With willing obedience, Miriam carried her mother's prayers in her heart and simply did what she was asked to do: stand at a distance.

STANDING AT A DISTANCE

Sometimes a mother's prayers are answered by sending someone else to stand at a distance and see what happens. We all know that meddling will answer no one's prayers. Neither will lectures. Standing at a distance sometimes means keeping your mouth shut and your heart ready.

If Miriam stood at a distance, imagine the distance Jochebed had to keep, staying busy during the day until Miriam returned with the basket and her son. Another day done, another prayer answered.

LIVING WITH THE ANSWERS WE HAVE

Can we recognize the partial answers to prayers in our own lives as hope-sustaining proof that God is working? Are we so bottom-line conscious that we do not see the answers that lift the load along the way until the whole prayer is fulfilled? I don't know if Jochebed was a worrier and wasted the answers to prayer that she already had. I do know that I have been guilty of such waste. Another day, another part of the answer. Carrying the answered parts of prayer in your heart is much easier than carrying the weight of answers not yet realized.

A MOTHER'S SUBSTITUTE

Miriam was a stand-in for her mother. Miriam's mother gave the care of her son over to her daughter. When a mother cannot be where her child may encounter danger, every mother prays for a stand-in. It could be a schoolteacher or church worker or Christian friend. It is someone who holds the same prayer for safety but is able to be close enough to the child without attracting the wrong attention. Miriam's mother could not be the one to watch her child. She would have tipped off the wrong people. Rather than protecting her son, she would have endangered him. Because she had no choice, she sent her daughter to do what she, herself, could not.

Miriam was a substitute for her mother, not a substitute mother. A substitute mother does what a mother should be doing. A substitute mother fills a gap that shouldn't occur. Miriam's mother did not abdicate any part of her motherhood. By sending Miriam, she extended her motherhood.

THE ANSWER WAS OBEDIENCE

Miriam did the job well. She did not wait beside the bulrushes to answer her mother's prayer. She waited there to be obedient. Her obedience delivered the answer. Because she did what she was told, her mother could rock and nurse her child with the sanction of the court.

Obedience always brings right answers. Often an answer that did not exist before appears on the other side of obedience. Looking for answers is not the same thing as looking for obedience. That's why we need to focus on God and not circumstances in difficult times. When we look to God, He always gives us something to obey. If we look to our circumstances, they give us something to fear.

WILLING TO RISK

Miriam was willing to take a risk in order to be the answer to her mother's prayer. Did she calculate the risk of defying Pharaoh's edict? Did the family discuss the pros and cons of what could happen to Miriam as well as baby Moses? When we read the story knowing the end, we forget that Miriam did not know "what would happen to him" or her (Exod. 2:4). She put her life in the same place her mother put her brother's basket—in the mercy of Jehovah God.

Heb. 11:23 reminds us that "By faith Moses' parents . . . were not afraid of the king's edict." The parents passed on their faith instead of their fear. For this reason, Miriam counted her risk negligible to the resources available through her Redeemer God. The hope, of course, was that He would save. But if He did not, He was Redeemer, the One who pays the price for release.

While prayers in times of crisis focus on rescue from danger or death, we forget that prayers to our Redeemer God link us with the possibility of release from fear and hopelessness and unending grief. Redeemer God is the One who brings us through even when He does not prevent. Miriam stood on the banks of the Nile, not knowing all of the risks, but willing to let her Redeemer have the last word about all of them.

A GENERATIONAL CONNECTION

A daughter brings a generational connection to all the mothers and daughters who have gone before.

While the mother is a direct tie to the past, her daughter is the line to the future. Passing on the generational connection is more than passing on trends and causes. It is passing on the essence of being a woman created in the image of God. The image of God fits every generation and every culture and maximizes God-created potential. Miriam's obedience was as feminine as it was expedient. She used her place at the river, not to fight for her mother's rights, but to build a bridge between an evil world and a righteous mother. Where can the daughters of our world build more bridges like that? And answer more prayers?

JOINING TOGETHER TO BE AN ANSWER

Miriam and her mother were together in their prayers to save baby Moses. The daughter provided the hands and feet for her mother's prayer. How that act of sisterhood must have cemented the mother-daughter relationship. Perhaps that is the greatest lesson they share with us. They focused together to save another. It was a mother's prayer that helped Miriam connect to resources she did not have on her own. It was Miriam, the daughter, who acted in behalf of her mother. Miriam could be her mother's answer because she was praying for the same thing. It was an unbeatable mother-daughter team.

Every daughter wants to be the answer to her mother's prayer. She does not want to be a substitute for the life her mother never had. Nor does she want to deny any part of her God-created individuality to become some icon in her mother's life. The daughter who obeys God has the greatest opportunity to answer a mother's prayer. Unfortunately, there are times mothers pray for their will and not God's. A daughter cannot obey God's will and her mother's will unless her mother has already submitted her will to God.

I'm sure Jochebed thanked God often for her daughter, Miriam. She was willing to go where her mother could not in order to save the one they both loved. It was a partnership that profited them both. Even without the implications that were to come, Jochebed and Miriam were joined by ties even stronger than blood: an answer to prayer.

Blessed be the tie that joins more mothers and daughters by answered prayer!

THE MOTHERS WHO PASSED ON THE GOOD NEWS

I have been reminded of your sincere faith, which first lived in your grandmother Lois and in your mother Eunice and . . . now lives in you (2 Timothy 1:5).

The story of the mother-daughter team of Lois and Eunice is the story of a faith relay. Lois raised her daughter Eunice in the Jewish faith. She passed on more than traditions of feasts and laws. She passed on a love for the Holy Scriptures. Little did Lois know that the most important prophecy of that Scripture would come to pass within her lifetime. A love for God's Word made each woman ready to receive the Word made flesh. We don't know when it happened exactly. Probably on Paul's first missionary journey, which included Lystra where they lived. What Lois and Eunice already knew about God's Word made them ready to receive more.

THE FAITH RELAY

Daughter Eunice continued the relay. She passed on the love of God and His wisdom from the Torah to her son Timothy. She didn't have to. Jewish boys attended school at the synagogue by the age of six. Using the Old Testament as textbook, they learned everything a Jewish boy needed to know about the world and Jewish law. But Eunice didn't delegate the religious education of her son to anyone else. She taught him the wisdom of Scripture "from infancy" (2 Tim. 3:15). You cannot teach what you do not know. Eunice learned well the lessons from her mother without the benefit of synagogue training. She built a solid foundation, which the *church* school continued.

Undeniably, the church needs to be a part of the faith relay. Sunday School, children's church, Vacation Bible School are all important factors. But nothing replaces or relieves parents from their place in the relay. In fact, faith only grows stronger as others join the race.

Of course, the real responsibility belonged to the Jewish father. In the case of Eunice and probably Lois, there was no *Jewish* father. Eunice married a Greek. Whether this Greek father believed that the Jewish teaching gave his son a larger worldview or whether he had died leaving the teaching responsibility to Eunice, we do not know. We do know that Paul, an exemplary scholar, praised Timothy's knowledge and understanding of Scripture. When he did so, he complimented Timothy's real teacher, his mother.

IN A SECULAR WORLD

Hers was a model of faith in the middle of a secular world. Eunice lived in a double-minded city. Although located in a Roman province, Lystra did not show marks of Roman sophistication. The people were superstitious and tried to worship Paul and Barnabas as gods on their first missionary trip. Then, with a little encouragement, the people stoned Paul and left him for dead. While there were pockets of Jewish residents, Lystra was largely a Gentile community. How Eunice raised her son to love God with all his heart, soul, and mind while living in a community that did not is an encouragement to all mothers. She taught him the Scriptures. She raised him with the understanding that the wisdom of the Scriptures would help him in all situations of life. Timothy did not add the Scriptures to his information of the world; he saw the world against the backdrop of God's wisdom. What a starting place! When he did that, he was ready for opposition, peer pressures, myths, secularism, or whatever anti-God philosophy might be floating around.

WITHOUT DIVISION

There was no hint that Eunice's faith divided the family. In fact, there is more reason to believe that the way Lois and Eunice lived their faith brought more unity than division. That does not mean they did not meet opposition. It means they did not allow opposition to divide the family. Over and over as I have answered teen questions about situations where parents do not support a teen's faith, even to the extent of making it difficult to attend church, I have counseled, "Do not make church or your faith a battleground." Battlegrounds draw lines and divide people. And whatever divides cannot unite.

CROSSING GENERATIONAL LINES

Grandmother Lois is a vital part of this faith relay that includes Timothy because, according to the only information we have about this family's line of faith, she began it. She faithfully passed on to her daughter Eunice the belief in Jehovah God. It was an applied faith that transferred to the next generation.

Principles of faith cross generational lines. Principles are the umbrellas that shade the generations of change from losing the essence of faith. Putting God first is a principle. The issues involved in that priority may change, but the principle does not. Children will always grow up in a culture different from the culture of their mothers. Passing on faith principles protects the essence of faith from secular, political, or philosophical bending. It is far easier to oppose or debate a rule than it is to reject a principle. Understanding the principles of faith protects faith in a way that legalism or tradition never will.

The model of faith crosses generational lines. We still look to heroes of faith no matter their generation. The stories of Abraham, Jeremiah, and Rahab give us flesh and blood examples that never lose their relevance. So do the stories of John Wesley, Jim Elliot, and Billy Graham. Everyone needs a model of faith to follow. We have no other description of the model of faith that Timothy followed except that his mother and grandmother successfully passed on their model to the next generation. And they did it at home where models always make the most lasting impressions.

Truth crosses generational lines. In fact, nothing withstands change better than truth. Take away the rules, and you better have truth left. If boundaries and standards and ethical practices don't point us in the direction of God's unchanging truth, then something is wrong. We may have opinions or rationalizations or good arguments, but we do not have truth. Truth clarifies and simplifies like nothing else. And truth lasts. That's the best thing about it. God's truth was the same when He created the world as it is today when any mother becomes cocreator with God and brings new life into the world. The model of faith begins with the truth of God. If it doesn't, it won't pass the generation change.

WHAT DOES NOT TRANSFER

Some things do not transfer through generations so easily. Tradition does not always make the trip intact. People who push tradition as truth have the form of faith without the substance. That's not to say that tradition is not important. Tradition is a backdrop for truth. When tradition comes from truth, then it shows how to reproduce faith.

In the same way, rules do not always make the jump from one generation to another. I can remember rules that my parents invoked when I was growing up that they did not pass on to my brother who came 10 years later. They were wise enough to realize that passing on rules was not the same as passing on faith. When the rules no longer protected faith, they changed the rules in ways that did not weaken the faith.

One radio speaker said it this way: "Rules and regulations without relationship lead to rebellion." The rule is not the protector of faith. A relationship with God is. Lois and Eunice passed on a faith rooted in a relationship with the one true God. When they passed on their relationship, the important rules followed.

CONTINUING THE TRANSFER

Not only did Lois pass the faith on to her daughter Eunice, but Eunice then made the transfer to her son Timothy. And somewhere in the transfer, mother Eunice prepared the way for Timothy to receive the gospel. By the time Paul arrived in Lystra, Eunice was a believer. It was no stretch to introduce Timothy to the message of salvation in Jesus. Her model of faith made it possible to connect to new truth. That's the adventure of passing on faith. It makes the next generation ready to receive direction and understanding that takes faith one step farther. It's the nature of the relay.

CALLED TO RELAY FAITH

How can grandmothers and mothers pass on the principles and models of faith to the next generation? Lois and Eunice didn't have seminars and self-help books. They only had the Scriptures. There was enough truth in what they had to give them something worth passing on.

And look at Timothy. He answered a call into full-time Christian ministry. He became a missionary partner, a "fellow worker" (Rom. 16:21) with Paul that linked him to the adventure of spreading the gospel to the Gentiles. Paul treated him as the "son whom I love" (1 Cor. 4:17). His birth father was not a believer, but God gave him a spiritual father in Paul. So great was the relationship between them that Paul wished Timothy to be with him when Paul knew his execution was near.

As mothers and grandmothers, we are still called to a faith relay. Some of us have been in it for generations. Some of us hold the baton for the first time. The essential ingredient is not the amount of people who have passed faith on to us but those to whom we are passing ours. It must be a faith that crosses the generations. This is the lesson that Lois and Eunice pass on to us: Receive the truth and pass on the truth in a way that makes it possible for the next generation to keep on receiving the truth.

THE MOTHER WHOSE DAUGHTER SUFFERED

Lord, Son of David, have mercy on me!
(Matthew 15:22).

Of all the mother's cries I have read in the Bible, none touches me more deeply than the mother Matthew and Mark tell us about. Jesus was on His way to retreat when a woman interrupted His privacy. Matthew identifies the woman as a Canaanite and Mark calls her Syrophoenician. Both identities mark her as an outcast in the mind of a Jew.

As if she were not already an outcast. Her daughter was demon-possessed. Symptoms from other Bible references include everything from convulsions, fits of anger to uncontrollable behavior. However this affliction presented itself, it separated the two of them from normal as the rest of their world understood it. No doubt they both suffered terribly from the stigma and isolation.

FIRST SHE HEARD ABOUT JESUS

How the Canaanite mother first heard about Jesus we do not know. She simply knew that Jesus was in town. No doubt someone had told her about the healings of other daughters. She wasn't looking for a healing or even a miracle. She was simply looking for help. How many other people and remedies had she already tried? Not enough. She had found no answer to her daughter's suffering. That alone was reason to keep following the leads.

This Canaanite mother was a woman on a mission. She was a woman with a need. Her daughter was suffering terribly. It did not matter whether it was a demon or a disease. Suffering is suffering regardless of the vehicle. No one feels a child's pain more empathetically than a mother. Every fever, every skinned knee, every rejection. Nothing wounds a child that does not also wound the mother.

HER WOUNDS BROUGHT HER TO JESUS

This mother's wounds brought her to the feet of Jesus. She brought the suffering to Jesus, not just a sickness. We may take our illnesses to the doctor, but we must take our suffering to the Deliverer. When doctor and Deliverer work together, wholeness returns, even in the presence of disease. Without realizing it, this woman had great wisdom in prioritizing her requests. Healing suffering involves more than removing pain and destructive physical symptoms. Fear burrows deep in suffering. Fear that there will be no answer. Fear that there will be no healing. Fear that robs us of trust. Where there is fear, there is suffering.

OBSTACLES DID NOT STOP HER

We find this mother at the feet of Jesus with her daughter's suffering. Even there, she encounters obstacles. The disciples tried to push her away, seeing this mother as a nuisance. Their focus was on bigger needs and other arenas. They were protecting Jesus, and she was keeping them from doing their job. No doubt they labeled her a neurotic. But no obstacle prevents a mother from pushing her way through if she truly believes that help is available.

I have been there—sitting in a waiting room hoping I would soon find answers for pain and suffering, only to feel a protective circle keeping me out. It was no personal attack. It was just that another person saw my child's pain without the urgency I felt. I've made my way past call-screening secretaries and relentlessly waited on the other side of closed doors to connect with someone who might have an answer to my daughter's pain. That's why I understand with great compassion what pushed this woman past the well-meaning disciples to get to Jesus. Perhaps the obstacles themselves allowed the woman to put her motives up against the roadblocks to see if they would stand.

Obstacles in the path of a mother's honest cry often increase a mother's persistence. Jesus said that persistence is a good thing to have. Is that because God doesn't like to answer the first time? Of course not. Persistence distills. It removes the unnecessary factors. It leaves the essence of the problem. And in this story it brought the woman's cry to the point where she could identify her core need: "Lord, help me!" (Matt. 15:25).

LORD, HELP ME

Does that surprise you? She makes her way, somewhat obnoxiously, to the feet of Jesus. Her first cry is for her daughter. But her second cry comes from her own pain. There is not a hurt, disease, or learning problem that my daughter has faced that did not also send me to my knees because "Lord, *I* need help." I need help to help her. I need wisdom. I need understanding. I need patience. I need endurance. I need creativity. I need compassion. I need help.

To be part of the answer to your child's pain you must first bring your own pain to Jesus. It is easy, too easy, to hide the raw edges of your own suffering behind someone else's. When you do, you push healing and release farther away for both of you. To be a channel for healing, you must first be healed.

TAKING THE PAIN TO JESUS

Is there anything that will take us to the Lord faster than our children's pain? When Band-Aids aren't enough to take away the suffering, mothers quickly find themselves at the feet of Jesus, begging. It's not that we have to beg Jesus to help. It's just that our cry must have voice. Whatever brings you to Jesus is not wasted. Coming to Jesus is always part of the answer.

She came to Jesus with her understanding of who He was. She called Him "Lord, Son of David" (Matt. 15:22). At least she knew who He was to others. While it may not have been the same as confessing Jesus as *her* Lord, she was well on her way. She understood that He had power. Coupled with her prayer for mercy was the desire that the One who had the power would use it to relieve her daughter's suffering.

JESUS RESPONDS

And what did Jesus do with her plea? "Jesus did not answer a word" (Matt. 15:23). I have been there with my child, hearing only silence after my cry. There are lessons to be learned in the silence. Lessons that only come from the silence. It is not an empty silence. At least it does not have to be. God's silence helps me examine the motives in my requests. His silence helps me to evaluate the level of my submission and makes me ready for true obedience.

The interchange that followed is steeped with symbolic language. Again, the mother shows persistence. At first Jesus does not answer. Then, when He does, His answer is vague. He compares her place in society to that of dogs (v. 26). Not to be put off by symbolism, she accepts the label and asks for crumbs (v. 27). She says she is satisfied with anything He can give. This mother knew what all mothers need to know. Whatever Jesus had to give was better than what she had now. Jesus called the woman's satisfaction with whatever she received "great faith" (v. 28).

UNDERSTANDING FAITH

Too many times we misname faith. We think it is faith if we believe hard enough that a thing will be done. And when we don't know if it will be done or feel the weight of logic and reality working against us, then we say we don't have enough faith. If healing is on the other side of having *enough* faith, then I can always have healing if I get *enough* faith. But isn't that just another way to stay in control?

It is only when we go where this woman went, to the feet of Jesus, that we understand how much power there is in a crumb from Jesus. The woman's faith was in Jesus. Her faith made her open to whatever He gave. Believing that what He gives is enough before experiencing it is faith.

IT ONLY TOOK A CRUMB OF FAITH

And from that crumb of faith—"Your request is granted" (Matt. 15:28). The moment of faith became the moment of healing.

This mother's cry reminds us to take our children's suffering to Jesus first. She teaches us to cry out to Jesus with all the intensity and passion there is in our hearts. Her example reminds us that we do not need to be afraid of obstacles or silence. She also teaches us never to neglect admitting our own needs. And always to realize that whatever Jesus gives is answer enough.

THE DAUGHTER WITHOUT A MOTHER

Esther . . . had neither father nor mother
(Esther 2:7, NKJV).

She was a foreigner, a Jew living in Persia. Her parents' family were among those forced to leave their native Israel. But they died. Maybe the adjustment was too great. Maybe a cruel accident or ravaging disease took them. Whatever the cause, they died leaving a child to be raised by someone else. Without orphanages and adoption agencies, children without parents depended on family members to step in. For this young girl, it was a cousin, Mordecai, who was by age more like an uncle. The girl's name was Esther.

MOTHERLESS

You've thought of her mostly as a queen, winning the country's first beauty pageant and spending an entire year swathed by oils and perfumes.

But have you thought of her as a daughter without a mother? Swept into the royal intrigue of one of the most fascinating stories in the Bible, we skip over the verse that described an unfortunate fact. She had "neither father nor mother" (Esther 2:7). Who taught her the facts of life? Who encouraged her femininity? Who listened to her secrets? Who played her pretend games? Even with willing substitutes, nothing is quite the same as having a mother.

My husband's first wife died of cancer, leaving him a single father to care for two-and-a-half-year-old Lisa. Lisa looked for a mother. She asked her grandmother to be her mother. She asked her aunt to be her mother. She even wondered if the nice waitress at the restaurant where they often ate would make a good mother. Thankfully, her father intercepted the invitation. Lisa didn't understand anyone else's relationship to her mother. She only understood hers. And she understood too well what was missing without one.

Esther did not have a mother when she entered the search for a queen. She did not have a mother when she entered the frightening world of the king's concubines. She did not have a mother when her life was at risk. And yet, while she did not have a mother or father, God provided Mordecai. He was her father figure and embodiment of mother-love. Making use of what she had, she found everything she needed. It is God's way of removing the destructive potential of life's unfairness.

COMING TO TERMS WITH LOSS

We don't know the age of Esther when her parents died. It really doesn't make any difference. We do know that Esther had to come to terms with what it meant to grow up without a mother. Surely Esther could not make the leap from Jewish orphan to Persian queen without successfully coming to grips with her past. King Xerxes would not have chosen a whiny, nothing-good-ever-happens-to-me woman for his queen. That means Esther had to make some difficult choices about her attitude and her circumstances.

Every motherless daughter does.

HEALTHY GRIEF

Esther could have believed that her motherless condition black-marked her future. She could have nursed her grief instead of nurturing her memories. Grieving loss is very different from reserving a place to keep grief alive. It is not a healthy grief that measures love by sustaining grief, as if the agony of loss keeps memories alive. Every grieving person fears this to be true. However, pushing through the grief like early crocus color, memories, firsthand and collected, contribute continuing links to a new life. Esther needed to celebrate the stories about her mother and to enjoy finding more links to the life her mother gave her without experiencing pain at every thought. Even for Esther this did not happen overnight. However, her story implies that it must have happened because the griefs of her past did not mar her future.

GOD STEPS INTO THE GAP

Perhaps the most important message Esther's story shares with us is that Esther didn't need a perfect set of circumstances in order for God to use her. Being without a mother did not damage her chances of enjoying God's plan for her. However, her attitude about it could have. It's easy to blame our present problems on what didn't happen or who we didn't have when we were growing up.

It is true that many daughters grow up without the nurturing mothers they deserve. With great compassion, God enters into the gap to create other sources for the modeling and nurturing any daughter needs. However, if we use our past to excuse our ignorance and destructive patterns, God cannot use His Redeemer resources. God is no less Redeemer in what has already happened than He is in what is going to happen. Only when we are willing to confront unfair realities as history but not as excuses will we be able to see Him bring together good things that do not exist in excuses.

GOD RECEIVES THE ORPHANED

One of David's psalms speaks to orphans this way: "Though my father and mother forsake me, the LORD will receive me" (Ps. 27:10). Many children feel orphaned in the presence of live parents. Whether the child is young or adult, living without the affirming attention of a parent leaves the child with an identity crisis. It is in these situations that God desires to fill the gap. He *receives* the motherless. He *receives* the fatherless. He is more than a substitute parent. When a child wants his or her mother, no substitute will do the job. A substitute only makes the child keenly aware of the loss. Instead, God shares himself as more than mother or father. He shares himself as Creator, Redeemer, Healer, Helper. He does not replace a missing mother, but He can replace the anger, fear, injustice, and insecurity with himself.

EMPTYING THE CLOSETS

If Esther thought it was difficult to live without a mother under the authority of Mordecai, it wasn't any easier within the strange and confining world of the palace. Any unresolved grief or attitude stood ready to explode with new grief in new circumstances.

Change has a way of opening up the closets. Perhaps that's why we fear it so much. A change of circumstances does not take away any of the ghosts or redefine any of the obstacles we set for ourselves. By changing circumstances we only give unresolved pain a new place to break through. Esther needed to enter the palace without unnecessary emotional baggage. She would need all of her strength and creative thinking to survive that secular world.

SUBMISSION IS A MATTER OF AUTHORITY NOT CONTROL

If Esther felt cheated because her mother died too soon, her story doesn't show it. Instead, we see her attitude of submission. She submitted to Mordecai at home. She submitted to Mordecai in the palace (Esther 2:10, 20). This was no weak-willed woman who had to be told what to do before she could act. Her very submission was an act of courage and strength, not weakness. Submission for the right reasons always is. When submission becomes a matter of control, it is not a matter of authority. Esther had already settled Mordecai's authority in her life. She understood that his authority meant wisdom and compassion and integrity and her best interest. On the other hand, control means power and competition and loss of rights. Haman, the personification of evil in this story, wanted power, so he exercised control and manipulation. Mordecai had authority and received obedience without coercion. It meant Esther submitted without losing any of her rights or personhood. By submitting to Mordecai, instead of challenging his wisdom, Esther protected her life even though at first she jeopardized it.

Esther found her strength, not as a daughter without a mother, but as a woman who did not allow her circumstances to dictate her predicament. When Paul found the same contentment, he called it joy. Not a feeling but a fullness.

MOTHERLESS TODAY

There are a lot of circumstances that take away the mothers we wish we had: death, alcohol, divorce, illness, or Alzheimer's disease. While each must deal with the grief represented in each loss, our attitude about that loss is the real culprit. Separating the pain of loss from its meaning for the future is the first step. Submitting to the right authority is another step. But allowing God to weave His redemption through the inequities and reversals of life is letting God have the last word.

Esther didn't have to fight her enemy; she only had to eat with him. Esther didn't have to fight for her life; she only had to expose it at the right time. God did the rest. Esther did not allow a mother's absence to prevent whatever God wanted to do with her. She learned everything she needed to know about womanhood and her personal identity without her mother close by. And the discovery process God used created a brighter future than she ever dreamed. While any loss changes the future, God always waits for our permission to redeem it. It is Esther's lesson for all of us.

THE MOTHER WHO LEARNED TO LAUGH

God has made me laugh, so that all who hear will laugh with me (Genesis 21:6, NKJV).

Surprise! The home pregnancy test told you what you didn't want to know. The doctor's visit confirmed your worst fears. You're pregnant. At the wrong time. At the wrong age. Knowing more than you wish you knew about the next nine months, you already realize that morning sickness and middle age are not a good combination. It's more than another mouth to feed. It's not even the 2 years of diaper detail that get you down. It's the way that a baby will control your body and your priorities for the next crucial years of a life stage that was supposed to mean more freedom. Add 50 plus years and you have Sarah, the childless wife of Abraham who had been promised children too many to count. What's there to laugh about when you have morning sickness at 90!

BEAUTIFUL BUT BARREN

Genesis introduces us to Sarah as a beautiful but barren woman. Others identified Sarah by her beauty (12:11, 14), but Sarah identified herself by her barrenness (16:2). Her beauty did not replace what she wanted most—a child. She would gladly have given her beauty if it would have removed her barrenness. Sarah never laughed about being childless. She found no humor in her humiliation.

HER PLAN BECAME HER PAIN

Sarah's pain drove her to take matters into her own hands. She resorted to a legally accepted custom of offering a servant girl to her husband as a surrogate mother to provide an heir. Soon her plan became her pain. She got what she planned only to find out it wasn't what she wanted. It is the hidden danger in every self-initiated plan. Hagar took Sarah's place beside Abraham and became the mother of his child. Sarah found nothing funny there!

ROLE-PLAYING

Twice Abraham used Sarah's beauty to save his life, instructing her to pose as his sister in the courts of two kings. Twice God protected Sarah and His promise. Only Abraham would father Sarah's child, God had decreed. But Sarah did not see God's protective hand acting in her behalf. It made matters worse when she witnessed God's healing of other women's barrenness. God had closed the wombs of Abimelech's wives and servants. When King Abimelech restored Sarah to Abraham unharmed, God restored childbearing to the court of Abimelech. Nothing makes a promise feel more impossible than seeing it come true in someone else's life. Sarah did not laugh at other women's pregnancies.

RENAMED

God renamed Sarah. Though the meaning of *Sarai* is unclear, there is little doubt that *Sarah* means "princess." God names her as coworker in the covenant. The woman who knows herself by what she cannot do hears God call her princess. Does it begin to heal her damaged self-image in preparation for receiving the promise? Perhaps. But still, no laughter leaves Sarah's lips.

THE FIRST LAUGH

It is not until Sarah is convinced that the promise will never come true that she laughs. Before this, the pain of waiting and wondering makes it impossible to see any humor in her circumstances. Eavesdropping behind the tent flap, Sarah hears the promise again from strangers. Now she laughs at the incredulity of such a happening. She laughs at the strangers' biological ignorance. She laughs because she is well past crying.

Finally, when she can do nothing to make the promise come true, the promise comes true. Sarah is pregnant. Can you picture her nine-months pregnant at 90? Now she finds true cause to laugh. For many years she cried because of what people thought; now she laughs and invites others to laugh with her. It is healthy laughter because it puts her circumstances in proper perspective. It is laughter that sees the humor in the similarities between a 90-year-old *new* mom and new baby—they both nap often, prefer soft foods, suffer blurred vision, and deal with incontinence. At the end of her life and the beginning of the promise, there is much more reason to laugh than cry.

WHEN THERE SEEMS TO BE NOTHING TO LAUGH ABOUT

It doesn't take a late pregnancy to put you in a situation where you think there's nothing to laugh about. Your teenage children can do it or a cancer scare or job layoff or even a move. Anything that threatens the security of the way you thought life would be is a potential joy robber.

Sarah learned that God's surprise brings laughter as well as change. She had already understood too well what life without laughter meant. Now, with a promise come true, she learned the value of lightheartedness. She knew that people were going to mistake Isaac as her grandson, and she learned to laugh at their reaction. She started seeing the humor in God's extraordinary sense of timing. She laughed at the thought of being the oldest *new* mother on Mother's Day. Laughed at the stretch marks that were lost in 90-year-old wrinkles. Laughed at how long it took to get down on her hands and knees to encourage Isaac to take his first steps. Instead of ending her life with the tears of what might have been, she ended it with laughter and with the enduring love of husband and son.

GOOD MEDICINE

Laughter is good medicine. Proverbs wrote the first prescription: "A cheerful heart is good medicine, but a crushed spirit dries up the bones" (17:22). The Arthritis Foundation recommends, along with daily exercise, that you laugh at least once a day, including one good belly laugh. Isn't it interesting that we pay lots of money for a drug to reduce or mask painful symptoms but will not give ourselves to the one priceless activity that has more healing in it than we may ever know? Laughter costs nothing, except a total reordering of our perspective. That's because whatever takes away our laughter takes away our balanced perspective. Restoring perspective prevents one circumstance from controlling the picture. It makes room for laughter.

In a seminar I attended, a grief counselor passed out red clown noses and made us all wear one. It is impossible to be serious about anything while wearing a red clown nose. If you don't believe me, try it. The red foam ball doesn't trivialize the challenges in life, it just makes you realize there's more to life than the fears and rejections and reversals that threaten to undo us. Maybe we all need to wear imaginary clown noses until we learn how to laugh again.

OUR CHILDREN NEED OUR LAUGHTER

Our children need our laughter. They will hear too many people laugh for the wrong reasons in their world. We need to teach them all the right reasons for laughing. Our homes need to be places where everyone laughs and laughs hard. We need to play together, just for the fun of it, without any thought about winning. Pillow fights, tickling tumbles, interchanges where we all end up giggling till our sides hurt. We need to be willing to laugh at ourselves first and always invite others to laugh with us.

A PRESCRIPTION FOR LAUGHTER

Decorators tell us to put something whimsical in each room to lighten the mood. It's a good idea for more than decorating reasons. Instead of formal-looking portraits, why not surround ourselves with family pictures that make us laugh? Why not put cartoons in the laundry room or near your least favorite cleaning spot? Share jokes and funny stories with family and friends each day. Surprise the family with something different—jokes on top of the clean underwear you put in messy drawers or a crazy picture in lunch bags. You'll find yourself laughing about it even before the family finds your surprise. Soon you'll find the same craziness returned to you. A circle of laughter is a good thing to keep going.

What would it take to bring laughter into your life? What would it take to allow an unexpected event that had nothing to do with physical or emotional abuse to bring laughter instead of dread or bitterness? What would it take to make you stand back and look at what you carefully planned and organized and say with laughter in your voice, "Well, I guess He showed me who's in charge"? And that's the key: There is more laughter in living under His lordship than there will ever be living by your own control and manipulation. Laughter restores the energy it takes to make midcourse adjustments. Laughter adds years to your life and life to your years.

Sarah learned how to laugh instead of cry. However, it took motherhood at 90 to do it. What might it take for you?